CHEF DIAMOND
Counts His Blessings

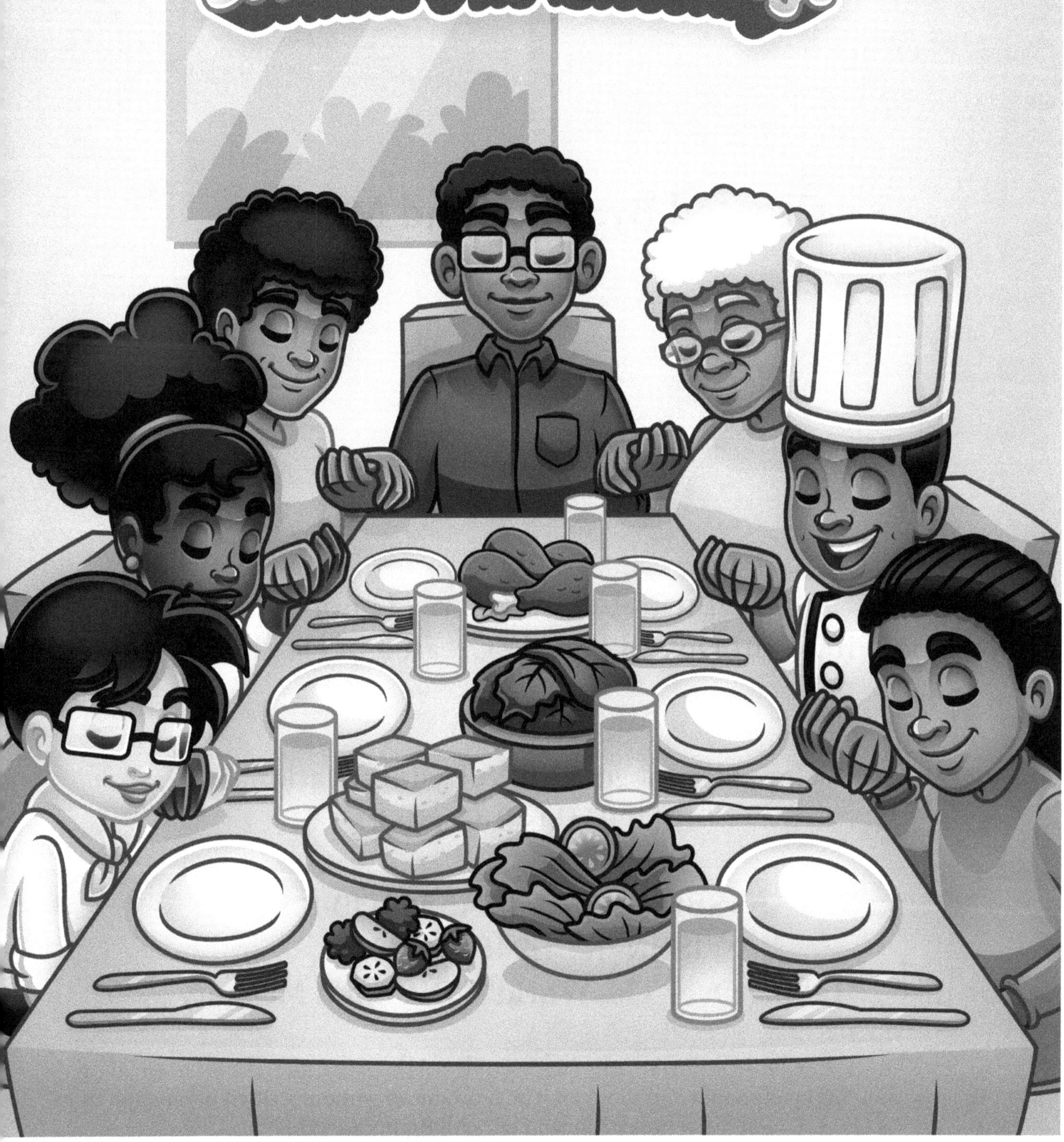

Created By: Diamond McNulty

Illustrated By: Harvey Lanot
National First Font Dotted Font — Created in 1994 by Roger White

Copyright © 2018 McNulty International
All Rights Reserved.

ISBN 13- 978-1-945318-10-8
ISBN-10: 1-945318-10-4
"Taking Over The World" - Diamond McNulty

Pages within this book cannot and should not be reproduced without written permission from McNulty International, LLC - All Rights Reserved

Hi Friend!

Join me while I Count my Blessings and you can count yours too!

- Chef Diamond

1 1 1 1

ONE ONE ONE

ONE ONE ONE

one one one one

one one one one

Chef Diamond is Thankful for Waking Up in the Morning!

2 2 2 2

TWO TWO TWO

TWO TWO TWO

two two two two

two two two two

Chef Diamond is Thankful for his Family!

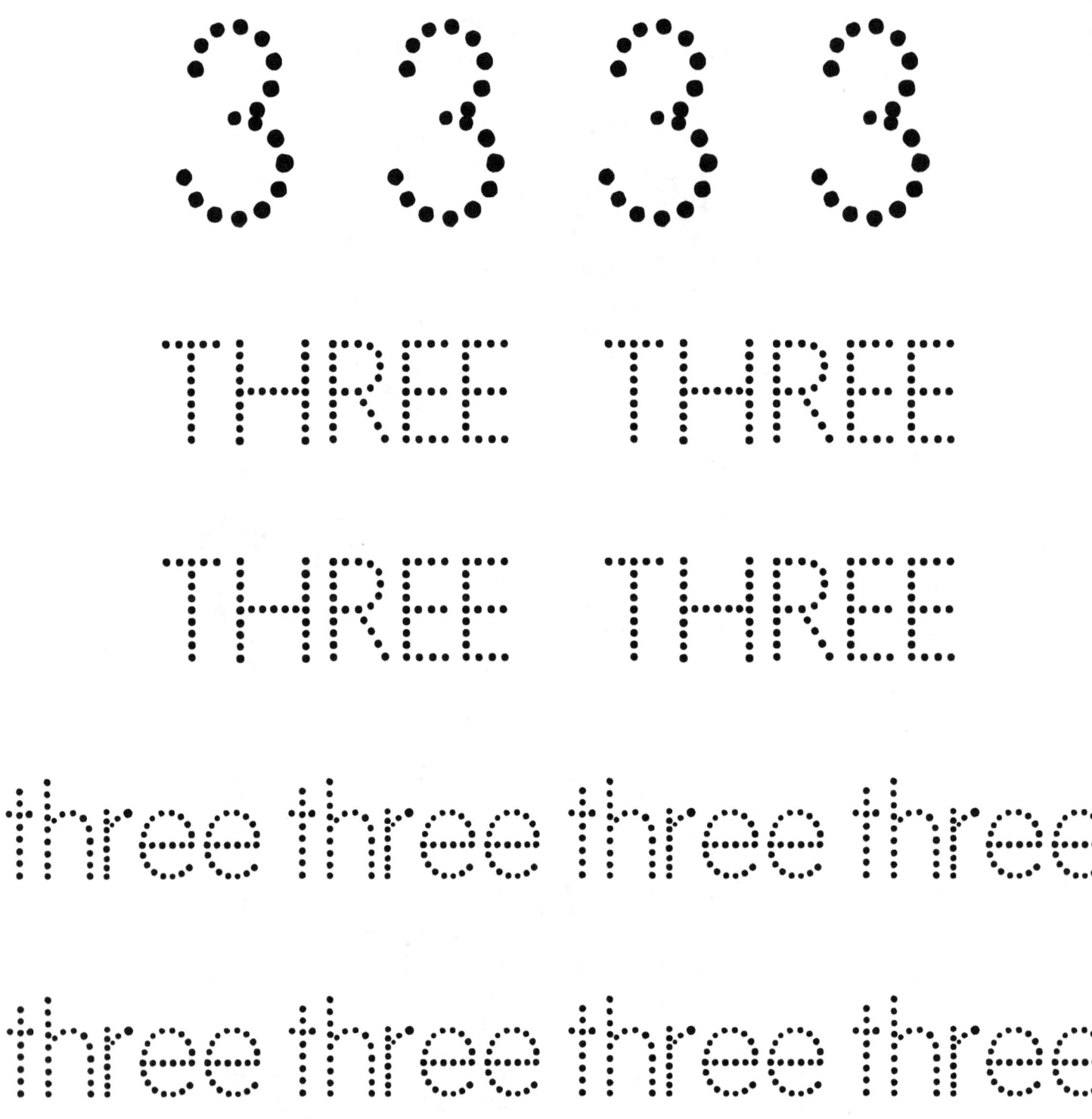

Chef Diamond is Thankful for his Friends!

4 4 4 4

FOUR FOUR

FOUR FOUR

four four four four

four four four four

Chef Diamond is Thankful for his House!

Chef Diamond is Thankful for his Food!

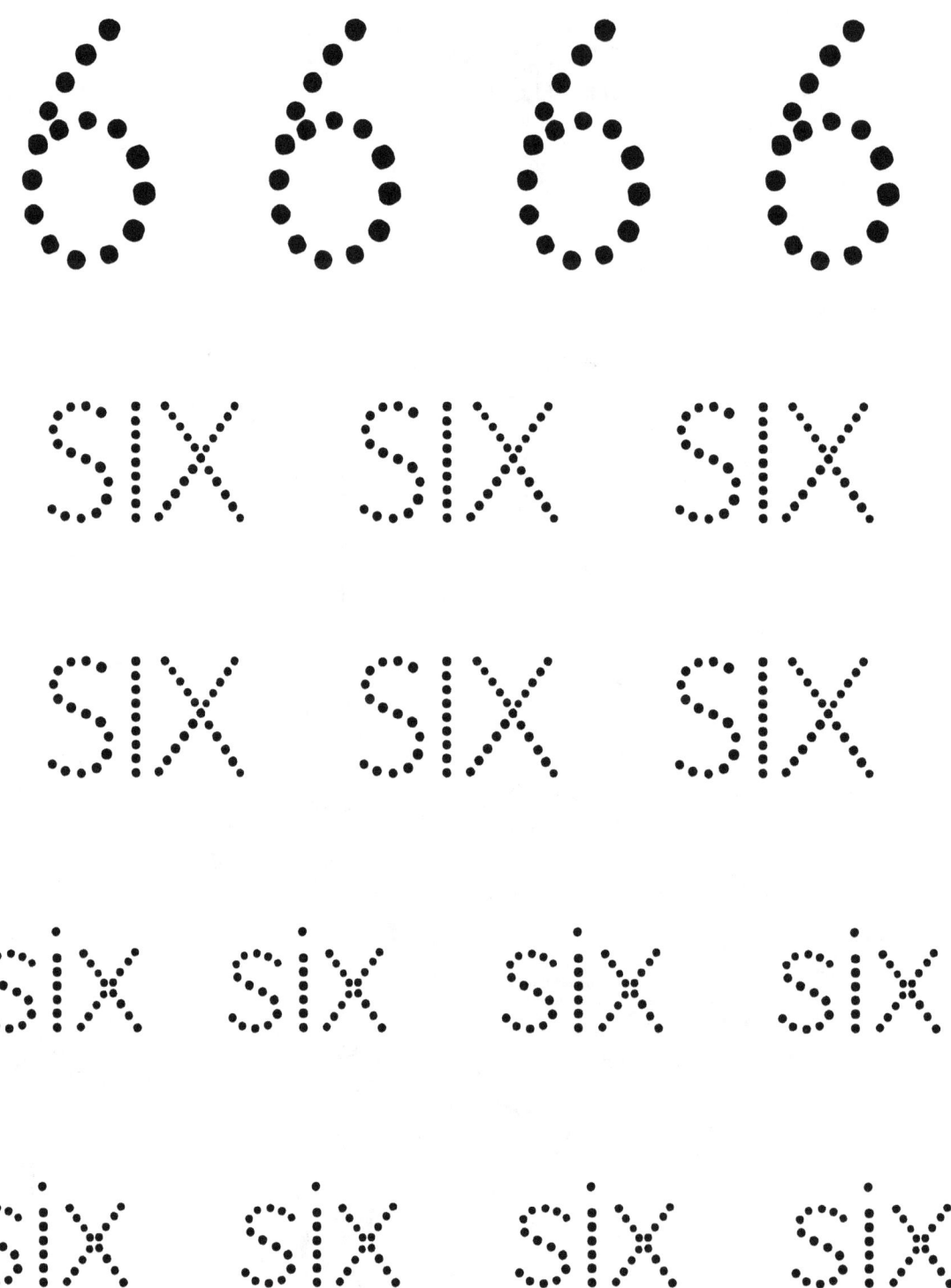

Chef Diamond is Thankful for his Good Health!

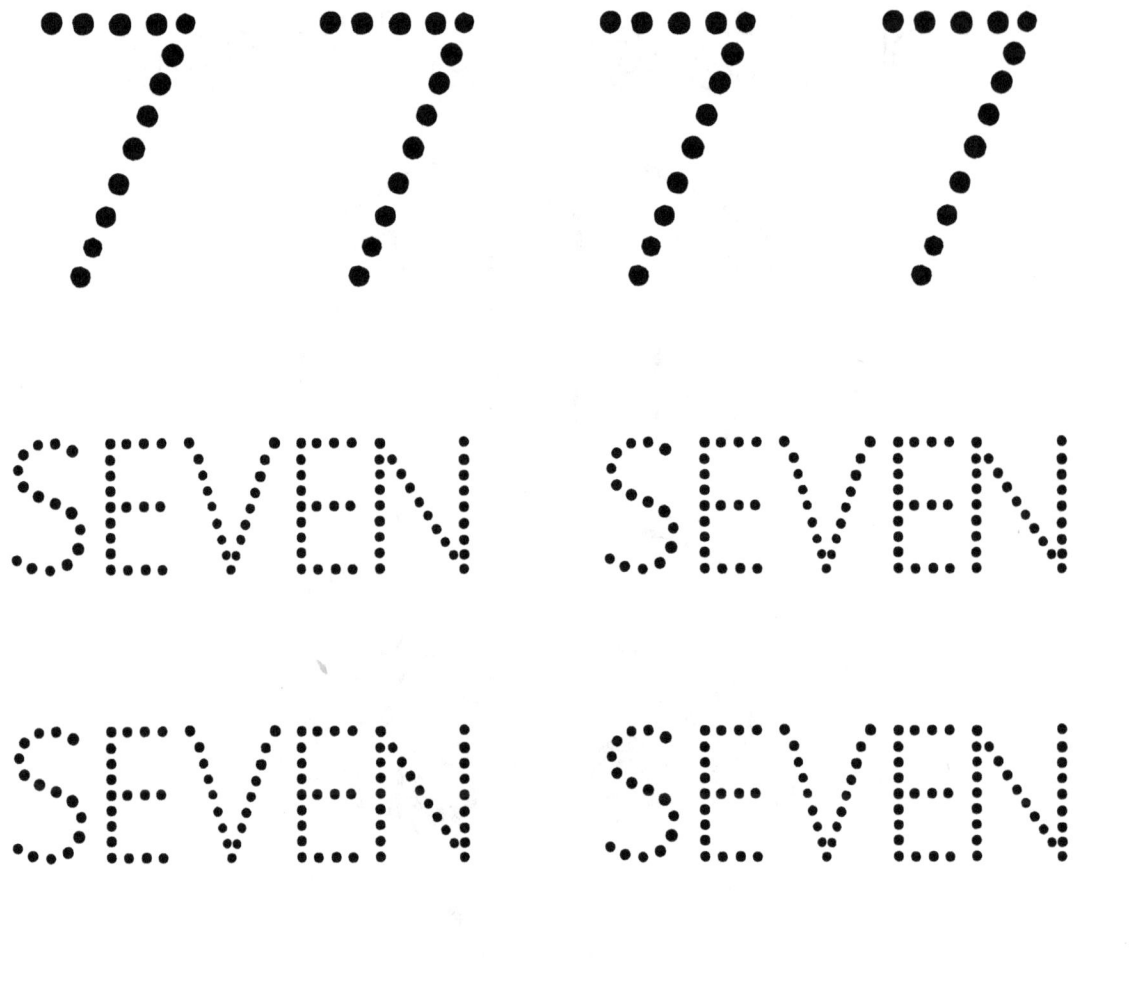

Chef Diamond is Thankful for his Clothes!

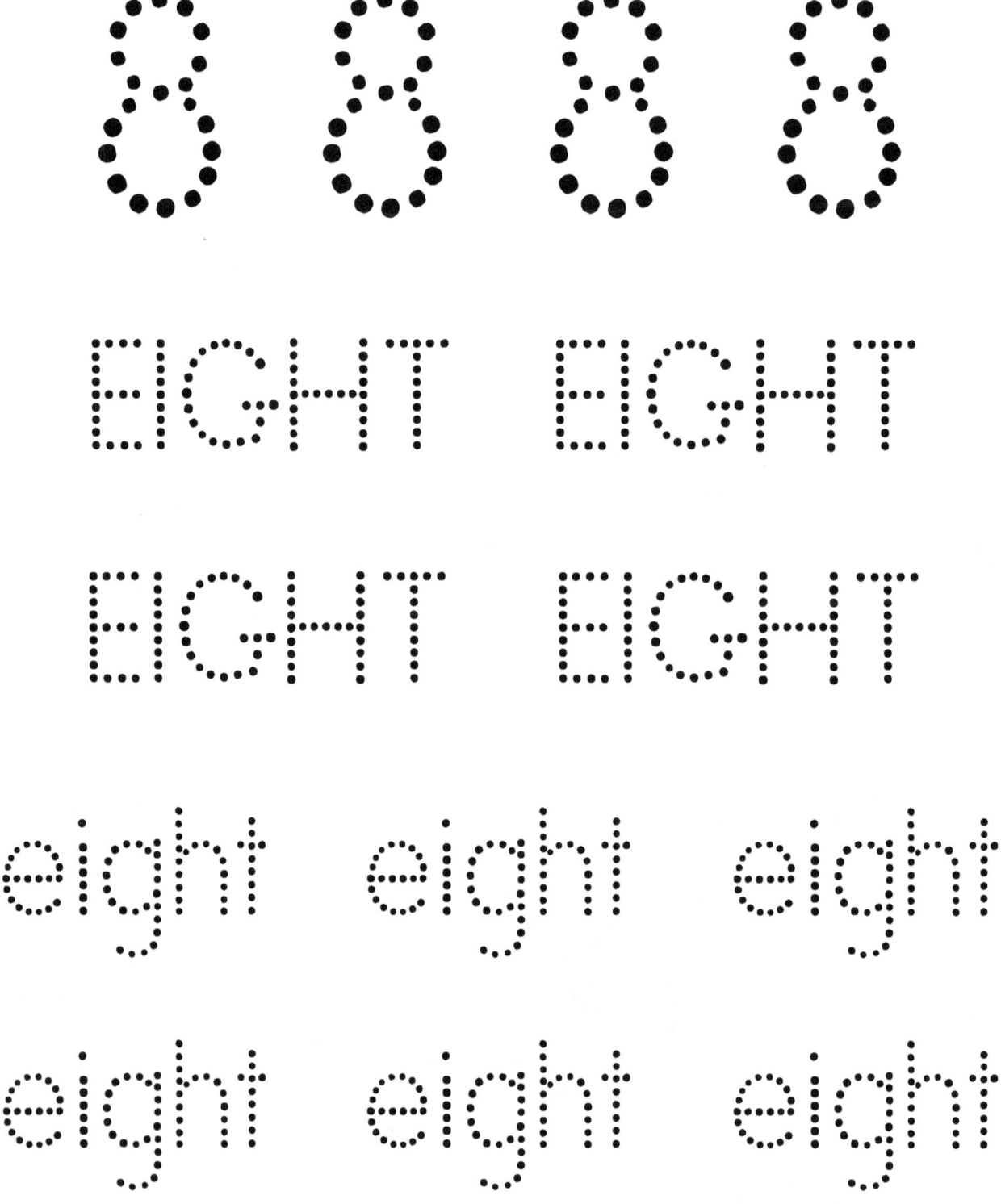

Chef Diamond is Thankful for his Pets!

Chef Diamond is Thankful for his School!

10 10 10

TEN TEN TEN

TEN TEN TEN

ten ten ten ten

ten ten ten ten

Chef Diamond is Thankful for his Church!

11 11 11

ELEVEN ELEVEN

ELEVEN ELEVEN

eleven eleven

eleven eleven

Chef Diamond is Thankful for his Mentors!

Chef Diamond is Thankful for Music!

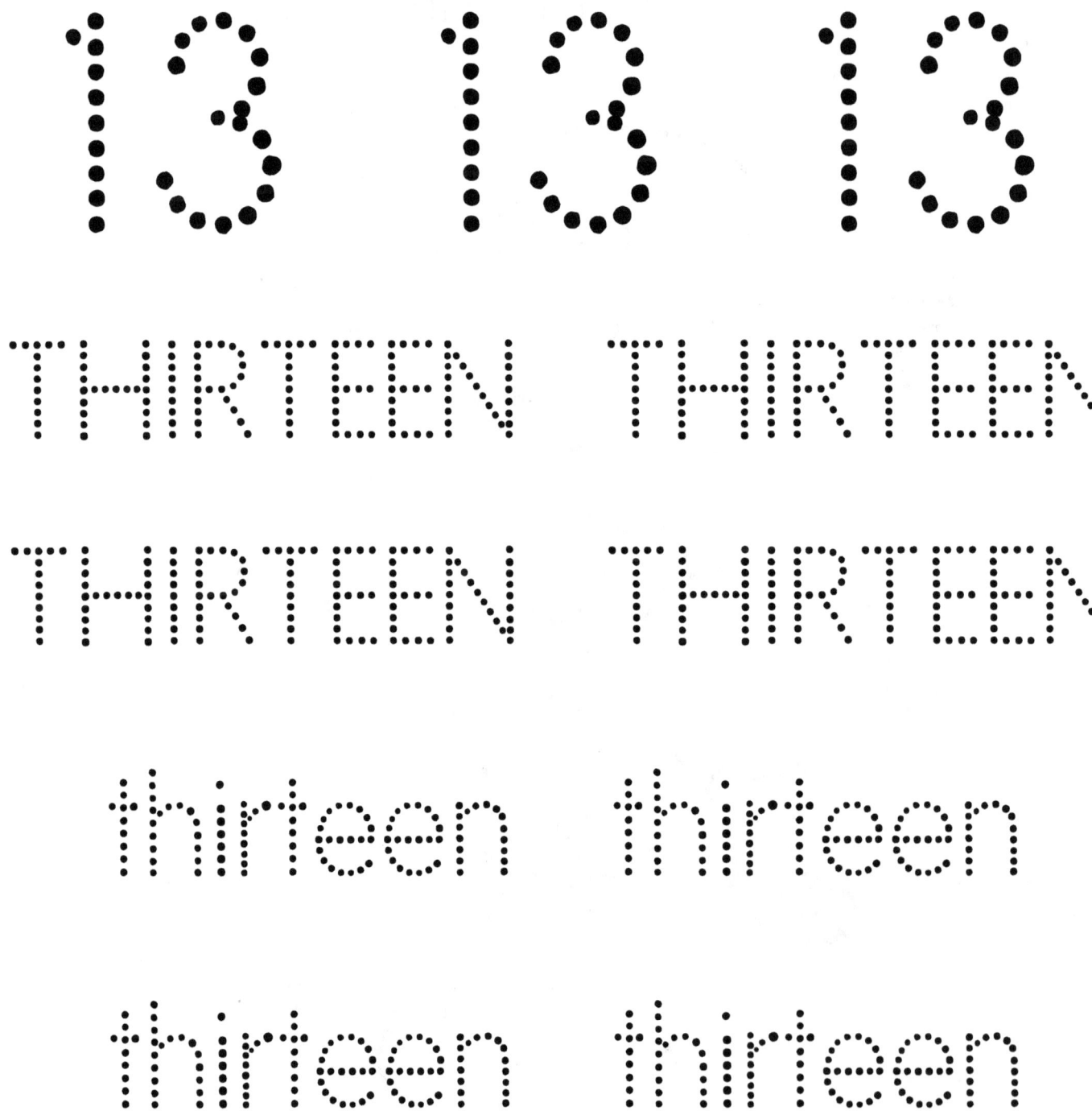

Chef Diamond is Thankful for his Vacations!

14 14 14

FOURTEEN

FOURTEEN

fourteen fourteen

fourteen fourteen

Chef Diamond is Thankful for his Toys!

Chef Diamond is Thankful for his Chores!

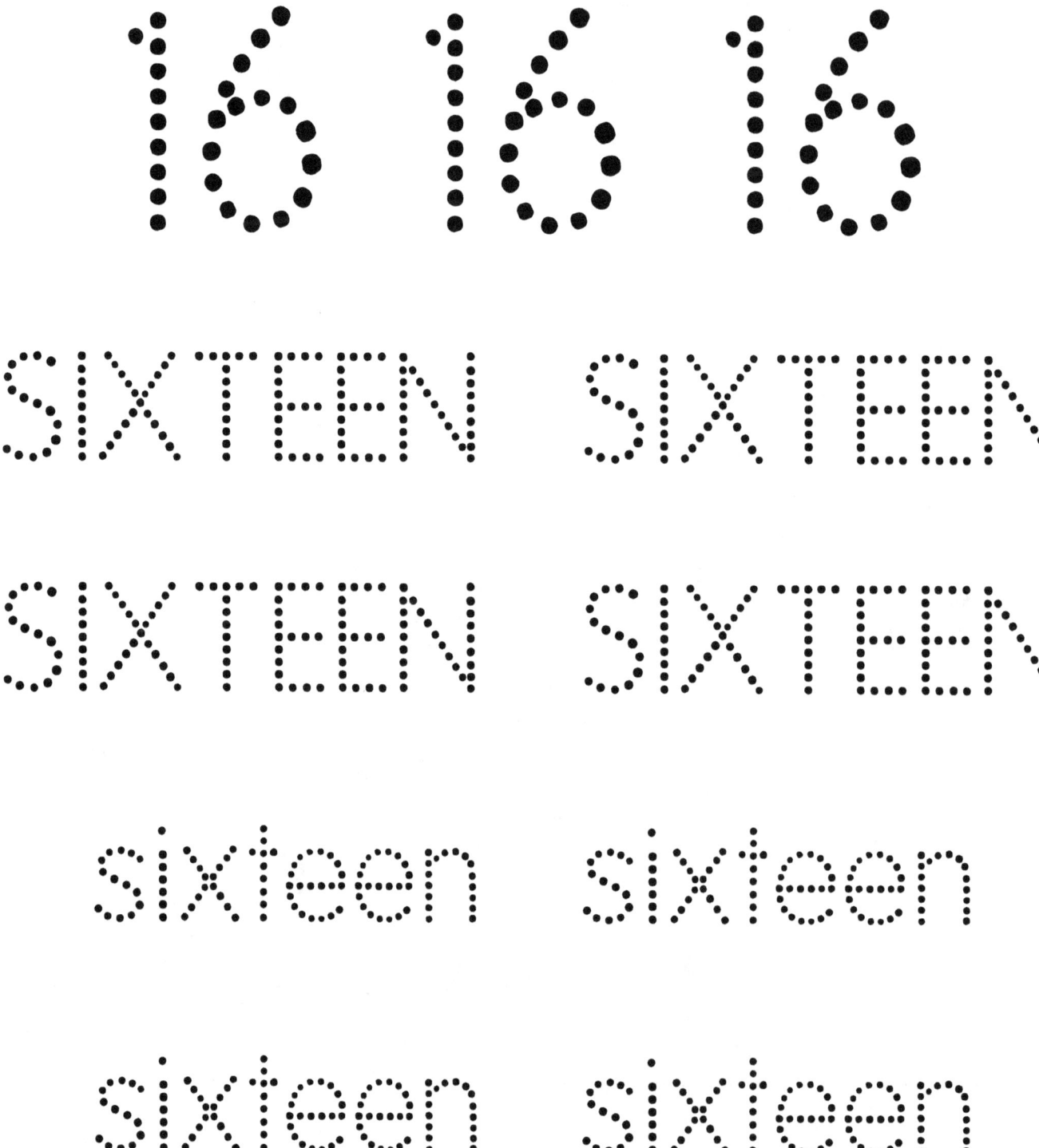

Chef Diamond is Thankful for his Playground!

Chef Diamond is Thankful for Nature!

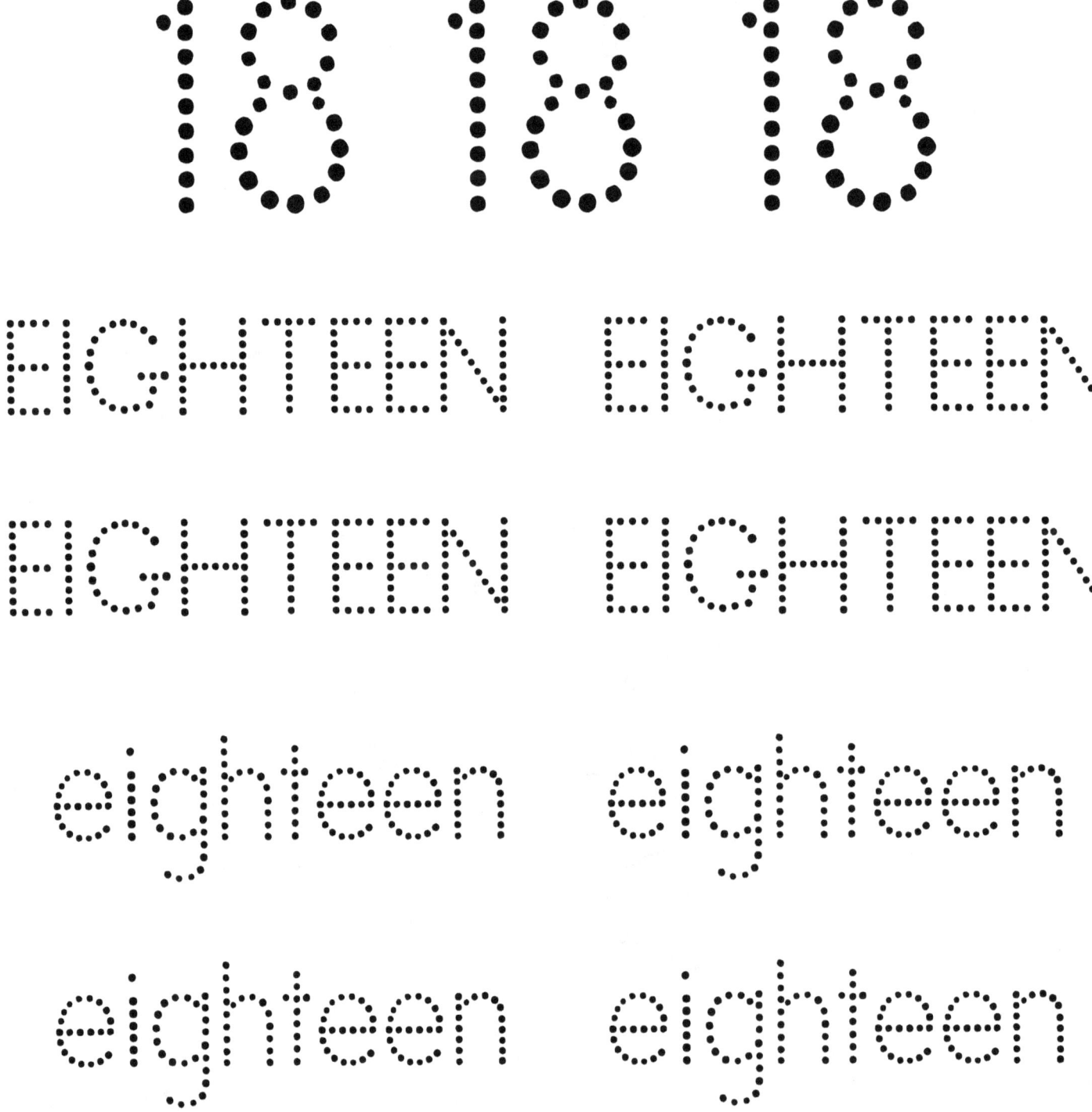

Chef Diamond is Thankful for Freedom!

Chef Diamond is Thankful for Love!

2020 2020

TWENTY TWENTY

TWENTY TWENTY

twenty twenty

twenty twenty

Chef Diamond is Thankful for you!

Hi Friend!

Can you name 10 things that you are Thankful for?

Name: _____

1. I am Thankful for _____

2. I am Thankful for _____

3. I am Thankful for _____

4. I am Thankful for _____

5. I am Thankful for _____

6. I am Thankful for _____

7. I am Thankful for _____

8. I am Thankful for _____

9. I am Thankful for _____

10. I am Thankful for _____

Checkout Our Other Selections Online at

Shop: Shop.ChefDiamondandFriends.com
Learn: www.ChefDiamondandFriends.com

Join Our Cooking Club:
CookingClubForKids.ChefDiamondandFriends.com